LEADING
— WITH —
TRUST

LEADING
— WITH —
TRUST

THE 12 ELEMENTS FOR ACHIEVING
PEAK PERFORMANCE

EMIL K. EVERETT

Advantage | Books

Published by Advantage Books, Charleston, South Carolina.
An imprint of Advantage Media.

ADVANTAGE is a registered trademark, and the Advantage colophon is a trademark of Advantage Media Group, Inc.

Printed in the United States of America.

10 9 8 7 6 5 4 3 2 1

ISBN: 978-1-64225-316-0 (Paperback)
ISBN: 978-1-64225-427-3 (eBook)

Library of Congress Control Number: 2024925573

Cover design by Analisa Smith.

This publication is designed to provide accurate and authoritative information in regard to the subject matter covered. It is sold with the understanding that the publisher is not engaged in rendering legal, accounting, or other professional services. If legal advice or other expert assistance is required, the services of a competent professional person should be sought.

Advantage Books is an imprint of Advantage Media Group. Advantage Media helps busy entrepreneurs, CEOs, and leaders write and publish a book to grow their business and become the authority in their field. Advantage authors comprise an exclusive community of industry professionals, idea-makers, and thought leaders. For more information go to **advantagemedia.com**.

*To my three boys—Colton, Dylan, and Hayden—
may these words guide you throughout life in leading
yourself and others forward.*

CONTENTS

ACKNOWLEDGMENTS

Throughout my career, I have been incredibly fortunate to work with exceptional people from many different professions, industries, and cultures. I am truly blessed to have had such rewarding experiences.

To my clients and program participants, you have given me many memorable moments. Your participation and contributions have provided valuable insights, adding more depth and meaningful content to my program delivery.

To all my colleagues who continue to challenge me and help me improve every time we work together—thank you for always bringing out the best in me: Kevin Lipomi, Peter Handel, Susan

Spader, Bill Bertolet, Fil Ionata, Darin Germanton, Regina Acosta, Ellen Oldfield, Fran Giambanco, Joe Armentano, Joe Cardiello, Robert Ranieri, Laurie Altschuler, Ryan Akins, David Green, Bill Lea, Laura Nortz, Jason Richmond, Cindy Benson-Delgato, Björn Höglund, Pilar Chaparro, Scott Fenwick, Jeff Schwartzman, Scott Laun, Mark Norman, the Crom family, the Escher family, Ercell Charles, Mark Pisani, Andre Hewitt, Andrew Terranova, Larry Heron, Don Schatz, Dan Ritchie, and Michael Frenda. This list could go on forever.

No words can describe my gratitude toward my mother and father. They taught me to dream big, value relationships, and push myself to improve daily. I feel truly blessed to have had them as parents.

To Jim and Bob, you have been the most supportive, caring brothers, always going above and beyond for me. Thank you for all your assistance and guidance over the years and for always being there for me. I am eternally grateful for your help in putting this book together.

To my three sons—Colton, Dylan, and Hayden—you inspire me to be my best, even when you drive me crazy! You are the greatest gifts in my life. Be good, do good, live it! My hope is that this book will help you learn to earn trust and lead others in the future.

To my wife, Karolyn, this book would not be possible without your love, time, and support.

I am eternally grateful to two family members whose lives forever shaped me: my grandfather Emil A. Kratzer and the Reverend Paul Everett.

Thank you to my friend Dianne LeVerrier for your proofreading and recommendations.

Thank you to Advantage Media Group for all your support in this effort, especially Harper Tucker and Joel Canfield. Also, thank you to the team that brought it together: Laura Rashley, Analisa Smith, Laura Grinstead, and Jenna Panzella. I sincerely appreciate your time, patience, and understanding.

THE BENEFITS OF TRUST

Trust is the glue of life. It's the most essential
ingredient in effective communication. It's the
foundational principle that holds all relationships.

—STEPHEN COVEY

On a beautiful fall morning in September, I brought my eight-year-old twin boys, Dylan and Hayden, to their weekend soccer match. As the boys ran onto the field, I realized their soccer coach was nowhere in sight. The other parents on the field were looking around, appearing as concerned as I was. No one had heard from the coach or knew whether he was coming to the match—he was often called away at the last minute to address situations with his construction company. To make matters worse, the soccer field was in a cell phone "dead zone" with no way to communicate with him.

With time running out before the start of the game, someone needed to step up and coach the team. As I stood near the goal, encouraging the kids to warm up, the program director, Matt, came over to greet me. As he approached, I could tell by the grin on his face that he was going to ask me to coach. I knew it was coming. So, without hesitation, I turned to my ten-year-old son, Colton, and asked, "Do you want to coach the twins' team today?" To my surprise, he enthusiastically replied, "Yes!" Matt and I both smiled at Colton's quick, eager response. With that, Matt agreed to delay the start of the game so Colton could prepare the team.

I turned toward Colton and asked, "What do you need to do to prep the team?" He immediately replied, "I need to warm them up. I need to get them to practice passing and taking shots on goal. And I need to get them into position." He accomplished it all in fifteen minutes and then coached the entire game himself. I stood with Colton on the sideline, acting as assistant coach. It quickly became apparent Colton had everything under control, and I was only there to ensure the other parents were comfortable with a ten-year-old running the show. As it turned out, they had nothing to fear—Colton's first coaching endeavor was a complete success, ending in a 6–0 victory.

None of this would have happened if I hadn't wholeheartedly trusted Colton's judgment and abilities and if he hadn't trusted my confidence in him to do the job independently. I didn't hover over him or offer any advice. He did it all on his own. My hands-off approach gave him more confidence in himself because of the well-earned trust I placed in him.

Through my two decades of training, coaching, and empowering individuals and organizations, I've learned that trust is the foundation for effective leadership. Trust enables team members to work collaboratively to achieve optimal outcomes and beat the competition. When trust is the main ingredient in the management mix, everyone works toward the same goals and objectives. As a result, they work in concert to attain desired outcomes.

Leading with Trust

In the best of times, trust creates impressive outcomes. In the worst of times, trust is essential to get people through a crisis. Trust is necessary for people to collaborate in order to overcome challenges, solve problems, and achieve common goals. The *Harvard Business Review* states that, when compared with people at low-trust companies, people at high-trust companies report the following benefits:[1]

- 74 percent less stress

- 106 percent more energy at work

- 50 percent higher productivity

- 13 percent fewer sick days

- 76 percent more engagement

- 29 percent more satisfaction with their lives

- 40 percent less burnout

Before we dive into the weeds of trust, consider these questions as you read:

- How do you create trust with your leadership?

- How do you instill trust in your business that will empower individuals to achieve more and make a more significant impact, professionally and personally?

---

1   Paul J. Zak, "The Neuroscience of Trust," *Harvard Business Review*, January–February (2017), https://hbr.org/the-neuroscience-of-trust.

Whether you're new to leadership or an experienced leader, I have identified 12 Elements of Trust to help guide you in developing and enhancing your leadership skills. These elements will help you initiate conversations with your team to identify areas that need more attention, enabling you to continue your growth as a leader. What can you do more, less, better, and different? What must you start, stop, or continue to do to strengthen your leadership? How can you become more intentional and strategic with every action you take as a leader?

Leading with Trust will answer these questions and provide the insights and guidance needed to help you create the type of leadership that drives greater trust and superior business results, regardless of how long you have been a leader. This book is designed to help elevate your skills and transform you into a leader with your own unique style. It will also allow you to face an ever-changing world with confidence and resilience.

The components of trust are organized into twelve elements that are explored in detail in the following chapters. These twelve elements are divided into two primary categories: elements that address character and those that address leadership skills. By mastering these elements, you'll quickly appreciate how you and your organization can use these elements to implement a "culture of trust" that will elevate your team and productivity to new heights.

In the first chapter of *Leading with Trust*, we'll explore the definitions of "trust" and "leadership" and analyze leadership "styles." Next, we'll outline *The 12 Elements of Trust for Achieving Peak Performance* as we start to discuss different approaches to becoming a trustworthy leader. In chapter 2, we will focus on the five "character" Elements of Trust—how they define you as a leader and how they impact others. Chapter 3 examines the seven "skill" Elements of Trust that are required, along with "character," to become a trustworthy leader. In this final chapter, we'll also introduce the *Three C's for Measuring Performance* to help you evaluate your leadership skills and progress.

Throughout the book, you will be presented with "Challenge Questions," setting you up for success in incorporating The 12 Elements of Trust into your daily routine.

Leadership built on a foundation of trust will allow you to achieve your organization's goals, and assist you in empowering the leaders of tomorrow. There comes a time when we all have to pass the ball and let others make their mark. That's what I did when I asked my son Colton to coach instead of me, and the result left me with a unique sense of pride.

I believe you'll feel that same pride when your team members achieve something remarkable after being empowered by your trust.

The ideas and concepts offered in this book will empower you to achieve a higher level of success and experience many memorable moments as a leader.

CHAPTER 1:

CREATING TRUST

*Earn trust, earn trust, earn trust. Then
you can worry about the rest.*

—SETH GODIN

"Do you want to sell sugared water for the rest of your life? Or do you want to come with me and change the world?"

Steve Jobs asked these questions of Pepsi President John Sculley to persuade him to join Apple as CEO. It worked. Sculley received a million-dollar signing bonus, another million in annual pay, and options on 350,000 shares of Apple. Unfortunately, what started as a great collaboration ended in disaster for both individuals.

When John joined Steve at Apple, they had a great friendship. Their trust in each other's complementary abilities fueled an incredible partnership for several years. Jobs respected Sculley's legendary marketing skills, and Sculley admired Jobs's innovative genius. However, over time, Sculley couldn't get comfortable with Jobs's out-of-the-box thinking and tried to run the business along more conventional lines. That didn't sit well with the iconoclastic Jobs, whose mantra was a tagline Apple would famously employ in a future ad campaign—"Think Different."

Conflicts flared, trust quickly eroded, and Jobs schemed to oust Sculley. Sculley soon found out and got the board of directors to remove Jobs from management. The upshot? After serving in a reduced capacity, Jobs finally resigned from the company he had created. But Sculley's win ended up as a loss. Apple employees lost trust in Sculley. The employees couldn't feel passionate about a guy who made his mark selling "sugar water." Instead, they still believed in and trusted Jobs's singular vision and commitment to creating distinctive products.

As Pepsi did with Coke, Sculley wanted Apple's computers to compete directly with PCs. That would ultimately mean gutting what was different about Apple. The company lost focus, and Sculley finally met the same fate as Jobs—having the board vote to replace him as CEO. Apple didn't regain momentum until Jobs returned to head up the company a few years later, demonstrating how achievement can falter when an organization's culture lacks trust as a critical component.

My favorite football team is the Buffalo Bills, even after the team suffered through a legendary seventeen-year streak of not making the playoffs. I know all too well that those problematic years were the result of inadequate leadership. As I write these words, the Bills are again at the top of their division—as their coach, Sean McDermott, says, "Trust the process!" In his first year as coach, the Bills finally made it back to the playoffs.

On a personal level, my experience playing college football at Wittenberg University first taught me what outstanding leadership can accomplish. Our team always ran out on the field confident of victory because we trusted each other and our coaches. We had a winning culture based on that trust, and that translated into optimal performance.

More on that story later, but for now, suffice it to say that trust holds a group together. Without it, an organization will invariably be pulled in different directions. Yes, people often give lip service to serving common goals and shared outcomes. Unfortunately, many people look out for themselves because they don't feel they can depend on others they work with—most of all, on their leadership.

The Nature of Trust

Before we go any further, let's take a moment to define trust. Trust is the belief that a person or organization is honest, reliable, and responsible. In a leadership context, trust is tending to relationships in a way that conveys respect for others and an understanding of their point of view.

Here's a brutal reality check—ask yourself, do you trust things more than people? Think about it. When you get in your car to go somewhere, you take for granted that it will start and take you where you want to go. It's the same with a laptop, smartphone, or other device. Unless the device has serious problems, you expect it to do what it was designed to do. If it doesn't, you're shocked. That's trust.

Trusting people, on the other hand, is a whole different story. People are complex beings with distinct personalities and motivations, which can make trusting people much more difficult than trusting your device.

Trust requires earning people's respect through skillful leadership. Sometimes, it's achieved simply by choosing the right words. When Alan Mulally left Boeing and took the helm of Ford in 2006, the auto manufacturer was in decline. Insiders questioned his ability to lead the organization because he was an outsider to the auto industry. His response: "An automobile has about 10,000 moving parts, right? An airplane has two million, and it has to stay up in the air."[2] With that one comment, he established his authority and made everyone at Ford more confident in his leadership.

But as we all know, building lasting trust takes more than words.

Trust takes time, especially in these volatile and uncertain times. Simply finding common ground is more complicated these days. The global communications giant Edelman does a yearly study that examines how much trust people have in societal institutions. Their research shows a severe lack of trust in business, government, media, and non-government organizations (NGOs).[3]

Each of us, at one time, has been burned in a relationship. Those experiences make us pause before

---

2   David Kiley, "The New Heat on Ford," NBC News, May 29, 2007, https://www.nbcnews.com/id/wbna18923357.

3   Edelman Trust Institute, "2024 Edelman Trust Barometer: Global Report," accessed October 2024, https://www.edelman.com/sites/g/files/aatuss191/files/2024-02/2024%20Edelman%20Trust%20Barometer%20Global%20Report_FINAL.pdf.

investing our faith in someone else. Actor Robert De Niro defined it so well in the comedy film *Meet the Parents* when he talked about the people he believed in as being in his "circle of trust." His circle included only those who had earned his trust and had not let him down or burned him.

Fortunately, skilled leaders have proven ways to complete that circle efficiently and effectively. Successful leadership comes in many forms and starts with your leadership "style."

Leadership Styles

Leadership is the ability to inspire, motivate, and empower others to produce desired outcomes more efficiently and effectively to achieve a common or aligned goal. How we manage every situation to get there can be different. There are an increasing number of established "leadership styles" used in managing the various situations you may face as a leader.

Situational Leadership is a methodology wherein you adapt your leadership approach across various leadership styles depending on the situation or who you're dealing with, be it your team or senior management. There's value in every leadership style, and a truly effective leader knows how to leverage each, at the appropriate time, to get optimal results. That's what Situational Leadership is all about.

The consulting firm Hay/McBer studied a random sample of almost four thousand executives and found there are six dominant leadership styles that impact company culture differently.[4] Let's briefly look at them and discuss which are most helpful in building trust in any situation.

COERCIVE LEADERSHIP

In a crisis, when it's "all hands on deck," coercive leadership may be the best way to move forward quickly. This type of leader asks for fast action without much discussion—they expect orders to be followed, not questioned. Coercive leadership can work well when the organization needs to solve an urgent issue. However, when an organization is not in an immediate crisis, coercive leadership can have many downsides. Opinions are routinely squashed, and individuals have no room to contribute outside the strict parameters the boss has laid down. Coercive leadership can have a counterproductive effect on employees if they constantly feel a level of fear or

---

4   Daniel Goleman, "Leadership That Gets Results," *Harvard Business Review*, March–April (2000), https://hbr.org/2000/03/leadership-that-gets-results.

resentment. That's why coercive leadership should be used sparingly and only when necessary.

AUTHORITATIVE LEADERSHIP

Authoritative leadership is generally the most effective of the six leadership styles. A true authoritative style is upbeat, fueled by enthusiasm, and most importantly, a strong vision. The authoritative leader uses these tools to mobilize their people toward achieving objectives and empowers them to do so independently. Individuals understand how their work fits into the "big picture" of what the organization is trying to accomplish. As with any leadership style, authoritative is not effective in all cases. This style can flounder if the leader is overbearing, pompous, or supervising a more experienced group.

AFFILIATIVE LEADERSHIP

An affiliative leader intends to create positive, personal bonds with their team members, demonstrating empathy to create harmony. While this is all good, an affiliative executive may lean on positivity and relationships more than results. A leader with this style may focus too much on avoiding conflict and not creating bad vibes. As a result, they may tolerate too much mediocrity.

DEMOCRATIC LEADERSHIP

The democratic leader tries to build consensus through participation. This leader needs to have everyone on board with the team's agenda. The possible downside with this style is the potential for endless meetings and discussions that delay action when required.

PACESETTING LEADERSHIP

A pacesetting leader is all about excellence—they demand it from themselves and their team. It is a particularly effective approach when time is of the essence. However, leaders who misuse it tend to badger those who are underperforming. When the underachievers don't start delivering at the level the leader expects, they are gone. Naturally, this erodes trust and can pressure employees to function abnormally and produce poor results. When team members feel expendable, it's usually for a good reason—the leader has acted as if they're expendable.

COACHING LEADERSHIP

A coaching leadership style revolves around helping people grow and flourish as individuals. These leaders help employees to develop personal goals and a workable plan. They will overlook once-and-done mistakes as long as the error helps the individual learn and succeed. Since this style focuses on personal improvement instead of organizational goals, many distrust the coaching style. However, studies have shown that coaching can positively impact results and employees.[5] Trouble only comes when the coaching leader runs into someone who has no interest in changing.

———

No executive uses one leadership style 24/7— leaders are particularly wise and most effective when they practice Situational Leadership and adapt their methods accordingly. In building a culture of trust, leaders will most often turn to the authoritative, affiliative, democratic, and coaching styles, because they aim to connect with individuals more meaningfully.

Alternatively, if a leader is interested in power and dominance, the coercive and pacesetter styles would be their preference. Of the six styles, these two should be used most sparingly. Sometimes it's necessary for a leader to lay down the law if someone continually fails to perform or a crisis demands immediate action. You *can* build trust with these styles when demonstrating your authority and

5   Chan Young Hwang et al., "Coaching Leadership and Creative Performance: A Serial Mediation Model of Psychological Empowerment and Constructive Voice Behavior," *Frontiers in Psychology* 1077594, no. 14 (March 28, 2023): https://doi.org/10.3389/fpsyg.2023.1077594.

demanding its respect, but constant top-down management can take its toll on team members.

The style that leaders use the least is coaching. Why? Because most bosses don't think they should invest that kind of time in a single employee. They believe the return on investment won't justify the effort. But the time investment isn't as substantial as they fear. Generally, setting clear expectations and having a few one-on-one sessions with an employee will get the ball rolling. And only quick check-ins, with proper guidance, are needed after the initial discussions. Even when managing a large team, connecting with each member on this deeper level is a powerful tool with a decidedly positive impact on culture and performance.[6] It's also potentially the best way to build trust. All great coaches know not to try to control the entire game—what leads to victory and success is the coaching of individual players. The players are the ones who are going to make great things happen.

Upon reflection on your leadership, do you rely too much on any one style? Can you identify previous situations when it may have been better to use a different leadership style to build greater trust?

Now that we've surveyed some leadership styles and their potential positive and negative effects on

---

6   Goleman, "Leadership That Gets Results."

building trust, let's explore some specific methods to develop trustworthiness.

Becoming a Trusted Leader

The *Harvard Business Review* identified four ways a leader can establish and grow trust through appropriate authority:[7]

1) BE WHO YOU SAY YOU ARE

Authenticity is all-important when you're trying to influence others. If you pretend to be something you're not, others will catch on quickly and think negatively of you as fake or insincere. A leader should always exhibit the values they are trying to promote in their own behavior. Mean what you say. Say what you mean. Live both through your values.

2) TREAT OTHERS AND THEIR WORK WITH DIGNITY

The more you consider individual ambitions and talents, the more your team will feel confident in your leadership. Create opportunities for your employees to shine. Invite individuals who don't have a high profile to take the spotlight once in a while. Consider

---

7   Ron Carucci, "Build Your Reputation as a Trustworthy Leader," *Harvard Business Review*, June 11, 2021, https://hbr.org/2021/06/build-your-reputation-as-a-trustworthy-leader.

individual aspirations and look for ways to link them to their role in the organization. Thank individuals for their excellent work and give them a safe space to fail (but not too often). Ensure you provide meaningful, positive, and constructive feedback that individuals desire. Otherwise, innovation and creative thinking get stifled. When someone does make a mistake, hold them accountable while keeping their self-respect intact. They want your positive and constructive feedback more than you realize—done so promptly and appropriately. Doing this will allow them to learn and grow from the experience and enhance their trust in you.

3) BALANCE TRANSPARENCY WITH DISCRETION

Anticipate situations in which you need to be discreet about confidential information, and set information boundaries. You can still open as many windows as possible, but withhold what you must—and don't make withholding information a power play. Steer clear of unsubstantiated gossip and never share something someone has told you in confidence without their permission.

Allow people to offer candid feedback or express personal opinions. At the same time, don't be afraid to provide others with the same candor. When a team reduces its blind spots and shares new information and knowledge, trust is strengthened through collective transparency.

Some business leaders advocate taking transparency even further. Ray Dalio—the founder of the world's largest hedge fund, Bridgewater—supports "Radical Transparency" in his book *Principles*. For Dalio, sharing all available workplace information, including mistakes and weaknesses, helps create an understanding that leads to improvements.

4) BUILD BRIDGES THAT UNIFY

Each team member brings a unique mix of talents and experiences that influence how they operate and approach their work. While your team may have a common goal, each individual will have different ways to achieve those goals.

To create greater unity, break down silos, and foster greater collaboration. Invite individuals from various teams, such as sales and marketing, to meet periodically and exchange ideas. Encourage groups to coordinate objectives and work together to identify new ways to achieve higher performance levels. Lead everyone to work for the greater good rather than isolating in separate corners.

On an individual level, take an interest in your team members. Understand what motivates them personally and professionally. Listen to understand and follow up on these individual conversations at a later date. For example, tie their motivations to the organization's needs or team goals and objectives. Put personal and professional motivators into context as to why contributing is essential. If you take an interest in others, they will take an interest in you. Everyone has a great story. It's your job to uncover it. That's where you can find commonality and collaboration, and build trust.

The 12 Elements of Trust for Achieving Peak Performance

Now that we have defined trust and leadership and have looked at techniques for building trusted leadership, let's break these ideas down further into what I call *The 12 Elements of Trust for Achieving Peak Performance.* These elements must be present to create a culture of belonging and achievement. Five of these elements relate to a person's **character**, while seven are based on **skills**. These character and skill elements represent the two primary means by which a leader can build, enhance, and restore trust to achieve peak performance.

Character is rooted in what kind of person you are, whereas **skills** relate to your ability to lead effectively. One without the other inevitably leads to an imbalance.

CHARACTER ELEMENTS OF TRUSTWORTHY LEADERSHIP

1. Motives
2. Values
3. Ethics
4. Credibility
5. Respect

SKILL ELEMENTS OF TRUSTWORTHY LEADERSHIP

6. Vision and orientation
7. Innovation and ingenuity
8. Strategic planning
9. Performance drivers
10. Emotional intelligence
11. Communication
12. Accountability

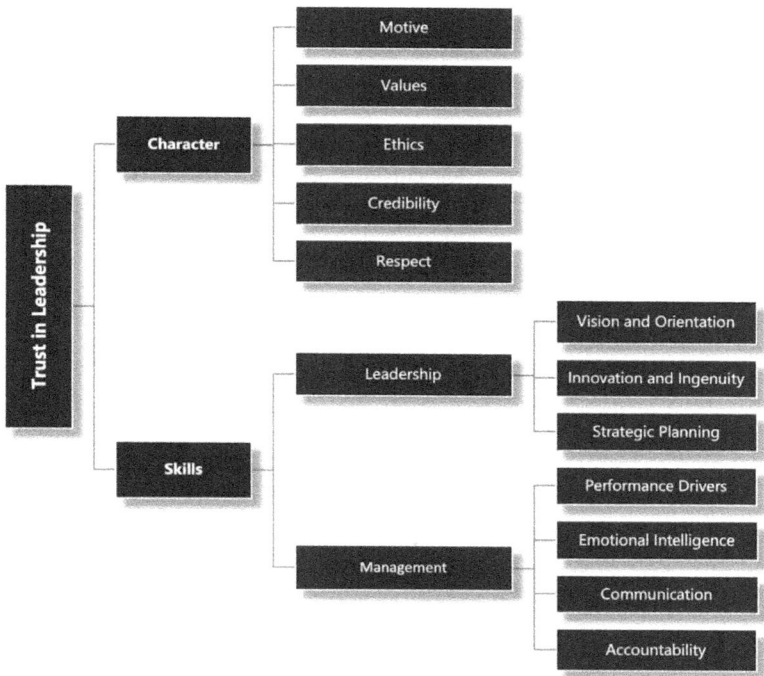

Figure 1: The 12 Elements of Trust, broken out into character elements and skill elements

You could have the most extraordinary managerial skills, but an emotional distance may be difficult to bridge if you're cold and indifferent to everyone on your team. On the other hand, you could be the most gracious person in the world, the life of the party, and have a kind word for everyone, but if your management skills are lacking, individuals will notice, and your leadership will suffer. So again, all twelve elements must be present to achieve peak performance.

While you cannot operate solely on skill or character, most of us have a tendency to rely more on one or the other for our success. Is there evidence that one yields better results? Sometimes, it's a matter of culture. For instance, some East Asian cultures emphasize getting to know someone before evaluating their skill sets. They trust a person's character and reputation more than skills, which is the opposite of what we typically see in the United States. Developing an emotional appeal and professional competencies is imperative wherever you live and work, as leadership requires balancing character and skill in any moment or place. How do you build better character and skills necessary for leadership? *The 12 Elements of Trust for Achieving Peak Performance* will help you do just that.

To assist you in evaluating your leadership development, we introduce the *Three C's for Measuring Performance*—Competency, Consistency, and Comprehension. This structured approach allows you to evaluate skills, sustain growth, and deepen self-awareness in your leadership development. The Three C's will enable you to measure and assess your success using *The 12 Elements of Trust*. Once you have fully mastered the Three C's—Competency, Consistency of competency, and thorough Comprehension of competency—you can become more agile in any situation. Optimal *Agility* is only achieved through mastering the Three C's. We'll discuss the Three C's and Agility in the book's final chapter.

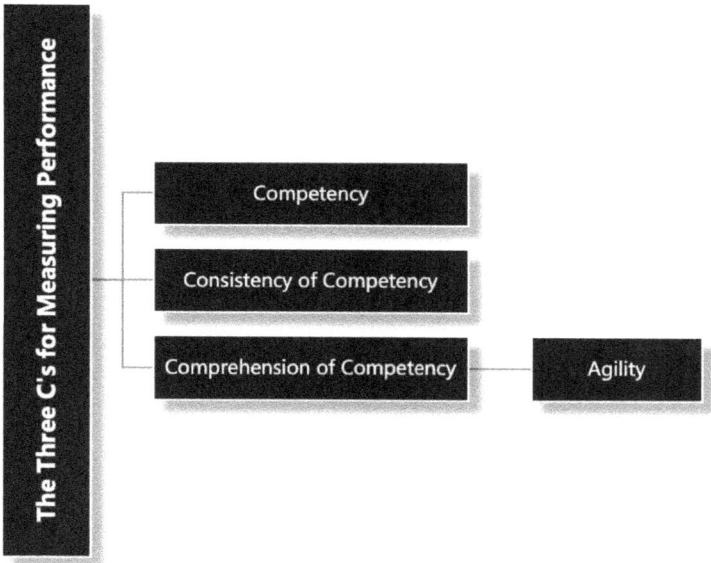

Figure 2: The Three C's for Measuring Performance

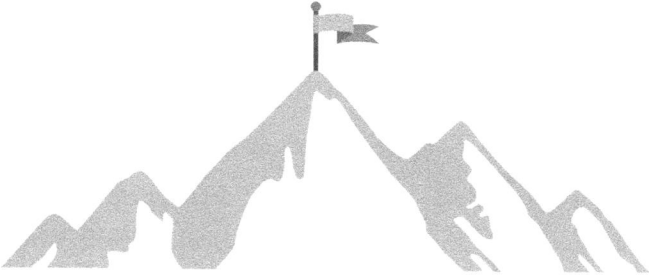

CHAPTER 2:

BUILDING TRUST THROUGH CHARACTER

Character is the foundation of all worthwhile success.

—JOHN WOODEN

The famous basketball coach John Wooden understood that an individual's character is the fundamental building block for achieving meaningful and lasting success. Developing and cultivating positive personal traits and values is essential for attaining worthwhile accomplishments in life.

Two colleagues I have worked closely with for over twenty years have taught me a great deal and have been instrumental to my success personally and professionally. Kevin Lipomi has been a key mentor, coaching me on how to train and help others perform at an optimal level. Fil Ionata has been a valuable colleague and friend with whom I have collaborated with on many projects. She is a remarkable person, and her candid advice and constructive feedback have been invaluable in helping me to succeed professionally. I never hesitate to seek advice from either Fil or Kevin because I respect and trust them both implicitly.

Seeking and accepting feedback from knowledgeable and trustworthy colleagues or friends can be invaluable for improving your skills and assessing your character. As leaders, we need trusted colleagues who know us well enough to offer objective viewpoints and informed advice that we can put to work. This, in turn, allows us to be our best for our colleagues, employees, and clients.

Kevin and Fil earned my trust years ago. That enabled us to be fully open with each other. There's never a question in my mind that they won't give me candid, constructive feedback to allow me to improve. It has taken time, work, and patience, but it has proven well worth it and invaluable to me.

Character counts, especially when it comes to trust. Kevin, Fil, and I share trust based on who we are—on our character. So, let's look at the Five Character Elements of Trustworthy Leadership—

motives, values, ethics, credibility, and respect—to help you lead better based on who you are.

The Five Elements of Character

It takes more than a title to inspire others—unless, of course, those titles include seven Superbowls, three World Series, or ninety international golf tournaments. What is important to us here is how these leaders—Bill Belichick, Joe Torre, and Annika Sörenstam—earned those titles. They were earned through hard work, determination, and persistence—in other words, through exceptional character.

You create trust when you are reliable, consistent, and positive. The following five elements of character and the accompanying *Challenge Questions* will get you thinking about how each element can contribute to your leadership style.

1) MOTIVE

Motive is essential to trust because it best represents your "why." Why do you do what you do? Motive represents your moral center and where you're coming from. Trust blooms if that happens to be a good place and aligns with the organization and your team.

Intentions matter. People will catch on when your motives are inauthentic, and you're trying to hide that fact. You can only generate trust and commitment to your leadership when you're as transparent as possible and committed to working for everyone's benefit.

Hidden agendas, for example, ultimately backfire and destroy trust. When a leader tries to get their team to do something for reasons they don't want to disclose, often to benefit themselves at the expense of others, it erodes trust. Hidden agendas use manipulation and outright dishonesty. These ulterior motives can't remain hidden. Someone catches on, uncovers the truth, and everyone sees the situation for what it is. Individuals will feel betrayed and lose trust. As a result, one who relies on hidden agendas will find it harder and harder to have an honest and productive relationship with anyone over time. It's always better to speak the truth and emphasize transparency.

Challenge Questions: What's *your* motive as a leader? Is it to raise the bar for the entire organization and seek genuine improvement to deliver positive results? Is your motive aligned with the values and vision of your organization's culture? Or, is it centered too much on your success versus the success of the organization and your team?

2) VALUES

Most organizations list their values on their websites or social media profiles. These values are the principles and ideals that guide proper behavior and business practices.

Creating a core set of values can benefit an organization as long as leadership recognizes that values alone do not inspire trust in and of themselves. Leadership must convert the values of an organization into daily behaviors and actions. Leaders must live and breathe the organization's values. Otherwise, they will look hypocritical, diminishing respect and trust. To quote Sheri Nasim from the Center for Executive Excellence, "Get your values off the walls and walk them through the halls."[8]

Leaders should model the organization's values and integrate those values into procedures, policies, and practices. Team members should be trained in those values, and leadership decisions should be value-based. Leaders should look outward at what's essential to their customers. What values do customers want your organization to represent? Are you following

---

8   Forbes Coaches Council, "10 Ways Companies Can Ensure Their Internal Decisions Are Values-Based," *Forbes* magazine, July 7, 2021, https://www.forbes.com/sites/forbescoachescouncil/2021/07/10-ways-companies-can-ensure-their-internal-decisions-are-value-based/247623c97fc4.

through on those values in your products and services? The biggest headache for an organization can be handling clients with differing values.

Strong and positive business values are becoming increasingly important to workers and customers. Millennials, in general, have a very negative and cynical view of "business as usual," according to statistics:[9]

- Only 48 percent of surveyed millennials believe corporations behave ethically.

- Just 47 percent think business leaders are committed to helping society improve.

- A majority of millennials worldwide agree with the statement that businesses "have no ambition beyond wanting to make money."

Demonstrating your values within and outside your organization's walls is crucial in today's business landscape, particularly when engaging millennials, who are rapidly dominating today's workforce as older generations retire. The statistics paint a clear picture of widespread disillusionment. By actively living and promoting your organization's values, you can differentiate yourself from this negative perception and build trust with clients and employees. To ensure your

---

9   Mark Emmons, "Key Statistics About Millennials in the Workplace," Dynamic Signal, accessed October 20, 2020, https://dynamicsignal.com/2018/10/09/key-statistics-millennials-in-the-workplace/.

values are focused and easy to remember, narrow your list to five or fewer to make them memorable. While promoting a shared understanding of a common goal is essential, remember that values guide everyone's approach to achieving those goals. Ultimately, aligning profits with purpose leads to greater success, not less. And having consistent and robust values in place is a great asset, especially when navigating VUCA times.

If you're unfamiliar with this acronym, it originated from the United States Army War College, which first employed it after the 9/11 terrorist attacks to describe the fundamentally different and unfamiliar global security environment resulting from that unforgettable tragedy. VUCA stands for:

- **V**olatility

- **U**ncertainty

- **C**omplexity

- **A**mbiguity

All four of these words clearly define the challenging times we all live in at this moment. The economic instability following the pandemic, multiple ongoing wars, and worldwide political tensions have made everything much more unstable. The business world has not been unscathed by all this change and instability. On the contrary, companies have found themselves rapidly adapting to sudden swings from what had been a relatively stable economic environment. We've seen disruptions in supply chains, shifts in consumer habits, ongoing accommodations to remote workers, and the rapid introduction of AI, just to name a few.

How do values help us deal with VUCA times? They combine to create a North Star that can guide us through change and provide much-needed consistency when it may be hard to come by in the marketplace. So show your people how seriously you take your organization's values—and they will emulate that effort.

Challenge Questions: Would people agree that your organization embodies the values it professes to hold? Would colleagues and employees say you represent the organization's values? What and how can you and your organization change to align behaviors with the organization's values?

3) ETHICS

Ethics differ from values in that ethics address the morality of your conduct. Ayn Rand defined the difference as follows:

> "Ethics is a code of values to guide man's choices and actions, the choices and actions

that determine the purpose and the course of his life. Value is that which one acts to gain or keep."[10]

When unethical behavior is rampant in an organization—and possibly even rewarded by leadership—everyone feels they may as well try to get away with whatever they can, especially when it's only considered unethical, not illegal. One only has to remember the Great Recession of 2009. Financial companies incentivized employees to take insane risks that led to the global economy's near collapse.

Think of being in a family where your parents lecture you about being honest and forthright, but you hear them regularly lie to others. Only two outcomes come from that environment—either you grow up losing respect for your parents, or you take on that behavior yourself. Either outcome is not good.

Fortunately, that wasn't the case in my house growing up. I viewed my mother as our family's moral compass, the bedrock of the family. Not only did she keep us in line at home, but she ran the family business. I witnessed firsthand how you can operate a company with integrity. She always gave people honest, sincere, and authentic feedback. Friends and

---

10   Ayn Rand, *The Virtue of Selfishness*, "The Objectivist Ethics" (Signet, 1964).

clients loved her for that, often saying she was like family to them.

That's how it works. The more you act with integrity, the more others will trust you. I was fortunate to observe my mother's integrity with clients and see its effect on them. Acting with integrity is crucial for trust and is a behavior I strive to emulate every day.

Challenge Questions: How would people that know you well view your ethics? Would people find you principled? Take note of your actions and words through the lens of ethics for a few days and see how well you do.

4) CREDIBILITY

Credibility is the quality of being believable. Say what you mean. Mean what you say. Don't muddy the waters with half-truths or rumors. There are two ways to gain credibility—either through your position or occupation or, better yet, by simply being your authentic self, demonstrating credibility through your actions, and consistently being honest in every situation.

People in positions of authority are viewed as credible simply because they've attained a certain title or status within their field or organization. People automatically view doctors, lawyers, CEOs, and politicians as credible, representing authority, and having expertise. This authority has very surface-level credibility and is attached to the title, not the person. As we know from millions of news stories, doctors are regularly convicted of malpractice, lawyers are disbarred, and CEOs are fired for wrongdoing. So, we must be careful about how much credibility we confer on people of authority that we don't know or have just met.

Remember, you can operate at a deeper level when your words and actions are honest, consistent, and reliable. You can accomplish more when working from a foundation built on, need I say it, trust.

This is why it's better to rely on personal behavior to create credibility rather than the power gained from your title. When you rely on your position or title, colleagues may nod and pretend they get what you are saying but then question it behind your back, especially if you've proven yourself untrustworthy. You risk losing time, money, resources, and respect if you rely solely on your position of authority.

Challenge Questions: Do you rely too much on blind trust? If the answer is yes, what kinds of consequences can occur? What do you believe others think about your credibility? Do individuals in your organization believe what you say and have confidence they can depend on it?

5) RESPECT

Respect is deep admiration for someone based on their abilities, qualities, or achievements. Treating people with respect is showing regard for their worth and abilities. As a leader, you show respect for employees by allowing them to shine. You don't micromanage them or force them to check in with you whenever they need to make a decision. Instead, you allow your people to pursue excellence on their own terms. This will enable them to develop a high level of self-motivation and self-determination, leading them to become more productive in every aspect of their lives.

The Wittenberg University football program has earned the respect of many. Wittenberg has won five NCAA National Championships, thirty-four conference championships, and over eight hundred games, making it one of the winningest football programs in NCAA history. My former Wittenberg coach, Dave Maurer, is in the College Football Hall of Fame, and his former coach, Bill Edwards, is also in the Hall of Fame. As student-athletes at Wittenberg, we had high standards to uphold.

In my sophomore year of college football, we made it to the conference championship. Late in the game, the championship title was on the line. We were in field goal range, with the score tied at seven, when the coach called on me. Surprisingly, I didn't feel stressed. When I took to the field, I was confident the attempt would be successful. Why? I credit my coach. Because I knew that my coach and teammates respected me and my ability to pull it off. I had no doubt his coaching had prepared me to make the kick. More importantly, I trusted that he and his assistants had coached the center to snap the ball accurately, the holder to place the ball down properly, and the blockers to keep the onrushing defenders out. I had confidence in my teammates to do what they had been coached. That fueled my spirit—because I respected them and their abilities. That put me in the zone. The ball split the uprights, and we won the championship.

As I ran out for the kick, nobody tried to coach me. The coaches had done that well before the game—not once, not twice, but a hundred times. The coaching came in the practices leading up to every game, when I was tired, when they were exhausted, when the sun was setting, and when it was cold. So, on that day when the clock was running down, they trusted me to do the job. As they say, it's the pain of preparation or the pain of failure.

Challenge Questions: Do you trust your employees to do their jobs, or do you continually second-guess them? Do you allow team members to achieve in a way that suits them best, or do you too often micromanage them? Do you give individuals the respect they require to remain motivated and engaged in their positions? Do you help set others up for success? In what ways can you show greater respect to those around you?

The Platinum Rule

Everyone has heard of the Golden Rule of "Do unto others as you would have them do to you." Generally, it's a good rule to follow, but it has limitations.

Sociologist Milton Bennett thought it could be improved. So he devised the Platinum Rule: "Do unto others as *they* would want done to *them*." Business consultant Dr. Tony Alessandra thought that principle was so good that he wrote a best-selling book based on that title in 1998. His version, "Treat others the way they want to be treated." More recently, CEO Dave Kerpen authored a book titled *The Art of People*, where he also cited the Platinum Rule.

"We all grow up learning about the simplicity and power of the Golden Rule," writes Kerpen. "It's a splendid concept except for one thing: Everyone is different, and the truth is that, in many cases, what you'd want done to you is different from what your partner, employee, customer, investor, wife, or child would want done to them. As great as it is, the Golden Rule has limitations since all people and all situations are different. When you follow the Platinum Rule, however, you can be sure you're doing what the other person wants to be done and assure yourself of a better outcome."[11]

Dale Carnegie, the legendary thought leader, was after the same concept when he told a simple story in his book *How to Win Friends and Influence People*: "Personally, I am very fond of strawberries and cream, but I have found that for some strange reason, fish prefer worms. So when I went fishing, I didn't think about what I wanted. I thought about what they wanted. I didn't bait the hook with strawberries and cream. Rather, I dangled a worm or grasshopper in front of the fish and said, 'Wouldn't you like to have that?'"

With that concept in mind, tailor your leadership to each individual when possible. Think about their needs, not just your own. And treat them fairly and with respect. Character does count when building trust in your leadership. Remember, a person's character is the foundation on which decisions and

---

11   Peter Economy, "How the Platinum Rule Trumps the Golden Rule Every Time," *Inc.* magazine, March 17, 2016, https://www.inc.com/peter-economy/how-the-platinum-rule-trumps-the-golden-rule-every-time.html.

actions emanate. Given that our actions are only as good as our skills allow, let's move on and look at the skill elements of trust for peak performance.

CHAPTER 3:

BUILDING TRUST THROUGH SKILLS

The toughest thing about the power of trust is that it's very difficult to build and very easy to destroy.

—THOMAS J. WATSON

When you demonstrate your leadership skills to your team, those skills inspire them to follow you.

Think about how the skills that people demonstrate influence your level of trust and behavior. If you have a regular mechanic, you've probably grown to trust them because they know how to fix your car. Hopefully, you have that same degree of trust in your doctor, dentist, or other professionals who have demonstrated their abilities to your satisfaction. Their proven skills repeatedly bring you back to them due to their competency and the consistency of that competency.

Strong and savvy leaders are no different. When they repeatedly demonstrate their capabilities, members within and outside their organization will trust them and take their actions seriously. Yes, character counts. However, character without skills can lead to disastrous leadership, while character with skills most often leads to outstanding leadership.

This chapter will explore the seven skill elements of trust, which are separated into two categories— skills for leadership and skills for management:

SKILL ELEMENTS OF TRUSTWORTHY LEADERSHIP

1. Vision and orientation

2. Innovation and ingenuity

3. Strategic planning

SKILL ELEMENTS OF TRUSTWORTHY MANAGEMENT

4. Performance drivers

5. Emotional intelligence

6. Communication

7. Accountability

Building on the five character elements from the previous chapter, the seven skill elements complete our *12 Elements of Trust for Achieving Peak Performance.* Each skill element represents a singular competency that leaders should strive to develop to build trust.

We'll discuss the details of each skill in a moment, but first, let's discuss the difference between leadership and management.

The *Harvard Business Review* distinguishes leadership from management in this way: "Management is about coping with complexity. Leadership, by contrast, is about dealing with change."[12] If we apply that distinction to a manufacturing business, for example, "management" would oversee the supply chain and ensure all processes work as efficiently as possible. If the market for that company's products fluctuates drastically, as we saw happen in many industries throughout the pandemic, leadership needs to step in to handle the change. "Leadership" represents the ability to go beyond the company's primary operations to navigate those changes successfully.

---

12   John P. Kotter, "What Leaders Really Do," *Harvard Business Review,*
      December 2001 https://hbr.org/2001/12/what-leaders-really-do.

The Three Skill Elements of Trustworthy Leadership

The three skill elements that help support strong leadership provide the tools necessary to deal with "big picture" change and disruption. These three skill elements are:

1) VISION AND ORIENTATION

Leadership is about setting the vision and orienting your organization optimally in an ever-changing world. An organization can paint a lofty picture, but it's only as good as the leadership's ability to understand the world around them. The first step in achieving proper orientation is to "get" the broad strokes of your organization and understand its place in the world. This insight lets you respond to new information with the proper context and mindset. Orientation makes it easier to discern what matters—and what doesn't. It will enable you to realign or reset the direction when necessary due to changes in the business and economic environment. Analyzing your environment allows you to increase trust because people will have more confidence in your opinion and your take on things. At the same time, if someone challenges your orientation with a fact-based opposing view, a good leader will take in what has been said and adjust their orientation accordingly.

Understanding the internal and external world around you is crucial to an organization's vision becoming a reality. Kodak developed the first digital camera and failed to seize that opportunity due to its inability to orient to internal and external factors. Orientation is vital to leadership because it's about gaining internal and external organizational awareness. A leader must acquire the answers to big questions about their organization before crafting or revising its vision statement, mission statement, values, and strategy.

Challenge Questions: What's currently occurring within and outside your organization? What significant social, economic, technological, or political issues are gaining steam that you must understand and address? Is what you see a new lasting trend or an episodic event? Based on this evaluation, what are the opportunities and threats to the organization internally and externally? How does this affect the organization's vision, mission, and strategy? What needs to happen to create change, given a new environment? What comfort level do you have asking others for their take on the current environment? What is your willingness to adjust your opinion if they offer new facts or ideas that could impact your viewpoint?

2) INNOVATION AND INGENUITY

Vision and orientation's best friends are innovation and ingenuity. Understanding your organization and the market it operates in is essential, but without innovation and ingenuity, you can not effectively prevail over change. This is especially true in turbulent VUCA times.

Innovation is doing or creating something that has never existed. Ingenuity is the ability to adapt or modify to an immediate, unanticipated event (the quick fix).

Innovation and ingenuity can be crucial to building trust. Suppose an organization does not exhibit innovation and ingenuity when a transformation is necessary. In this case, employees may perceive it as an inability to pivot effectively and will likely lose confidence. Whenever significant change comes to an organization or industry, individuals often feel overwhelmed and stressed out, believing leadership won't be able to handle it.

Whether or not you possess an inspired sense of innovation and ingenuity, you can draw upon others inside and outside the organization for help and guidance. As a result, solutions will be created, and trust will grow in challenging environments.

Challenge Questions: How do you encourage people to think outside the box when tackling a complex problem? How do you implement new ways of doing things when change is required? Do you see your organization as an ever-evolving entity that must continue to innovate and grow to stay relevant? In what ways can you keep your organization transformational?

3) STRATEGIC PLANNING

Vision, orientation, innovation, and ingenuity are preludes to strategic planning and creating a detailed road map to an improved future for the organization. How you plan strategically, while guided by solid values, can determine your ability to build and gain more trust.

Strategic planning is the art of developing detailed strategies, implementing those strategies, and evaluating the processes used in executing the plan to achieve the organization's vision and mission. A coordinated planning process best utilizes the organization's time, money, and resources.

As a leader, the more you include others in the strategic planning process, the more they will invest in its fulfillment. If they are involved in the process, they will own it. Confidence in your ability to plan strategically will build trust, and you will ultimately be more successful.

Trust can also be enhanced when your strategic planning process is flexible enough to meet today's ever-changing world. A simple four-step process can go a long way in helping you become more agile. Air Force Colonel John Boyd developed the OODA Loop to help pilots deal with unpredictable situations:

1. **O**bserve what's going on.

2. **O**rient yourself to the environment.

3. **D**ecide on a course of action.

4. **A**ct to implement your plan.

The OODA Loop is a concise and effective way to approach strategic planning. By framing it as an endless loop, you allow your plan to be more adaptive in volatile environments.

Challenge Questions: What is your strategic planning methodology? Is there transparency and diversity of thought in the process? Do you allow critical thinking? Do you stress-test your strategic plans? How flexible is your strategic planning process in an ever-changing environment, and how agile is your organization? Based on your observations and input from others, what needs to be added to your strategic planning process?

The Four Skill Elements of Trustworthy Management

The skill elements of leadership we just covered create a framework for leading change, moving the organization forward, and laying out concrete steps to achieve a vision.

In contrast, the skill elements of management are about execution—getting things done. As any business person knows, plans stay plans and are never transformed into reality without the ability to execute. These four elements of execution ensure your agendas become a reality. They are drivers of implementation and accomplishment and are just as crucial as the skill elements of leadership.

1) PERFORMANCE DRIVERS

Are the individuals in your organization working efficiently and effectively as a team toward a shared outcome? Or are they just going through the motions and making excuses?

Performance drivers are the skills and specific processes you utilize to produce desired outcomes efficiently. The methods within these skills will bring out the best in your team members. When executed correctly, you can create a culture that allows individuals to grow, be engaged, and feel respected.

Examples of the key performance drivers include:

- Tactical planning, project management, and goal setting

- Individual and team development

- Time and team management

- Critical thinking and problem-solving

- Decision-making

- Delegation

- Coaching

- Advice, feedback, recognition, and appreciation

- Change and crisis management

- Conflict management

- Negotiating

- Networking

Challenge questions: Which performance drivers can you implement or improve to build greater trust with your colleagues? Which performance drivers need the most attention to drive greater productivity?

When did you last work on enhancing your skills to improve performance?

2) EMOTIONAL INTELLIGENCE

Emotional intelligence (EI) is related to orientation but focuses on people. While orientation is understanding your organization internally and externally, having emotional intelligence is knowing yourself and the people around you. With EI, you are aware of your personality and how it impacts others—and you're also mindful of others. You understand a person's personality and can easily demonstrate the appropriate emotion depending on the person and the situation. You know how to connect with individuals and get the best out of them through respectful interactions.

Leadership is challenging if you lack the skills to bond with others. Developing EI helps you build the needed trust in who you are, which opens the door to creating genuine and strong relationships. With EI in place, you possess self-awareness, self-management, social awareness, and social skills. You can use all these tools to expand your leadership and create professional bonds that breed respect and trust. You're also able to control your own negative emotions with more composure. You're still a human being of course, but through EI you learn how to cool down before saying something you may regret. As Tim Grover, the author of *Winning*, stated, "Control your thoughts, you control your emotions."

EI should be an essential component in every aspect of your life. As a leader, EI is critical to your ability to build a powerful organization and lead it to the next level.

Challenge Questions: Is EI something you practice daily or occasionally in your leadership role? Is EI encouraged in your organization? Are you aware of others' needs, and do you provide mentorship and support when needed?

3) COMMUNICATION

Good communication skills are the keystone for building trust as a leader. When you excel at communication, everyone knows where you stand. You communicate your intent and strategy, provide and accept feedback, and promptly address questions, concerns, and general comments. As a good communicator, you're present and engaged in your interactions—your verbal and non-verbal cues are in sync. You share stories to engage others. And you are constantly making it a point to listen when others speak, *really* listening to what the other person is saying.

The best communicators are primarily great listeners, listening to understand versus listening to respond.

Communication falters when you are not sincere and open. While it's true that business leaders can't always disclose everything that's happening in the company, you should still strive to approach people from a foundation of truth whenever possible. That means avoiding excessive sugarcoating or trying to please everyone you talk to. It also means avoiding the other extreme—where you always seem in crisis mode, and as a result, you make others feel edgy and nervous.

How you communicate drives results. Review your communications periodically to see how you can improve and create greater engagement with your team. Also, protocols and guidelines for internal and external communications should be considered. They can help keep communication focused and consistent and lighten your inbox.

Challenge Questions: When did you last take a step back to analyze how you communicate with those around you? Are your written communications cold and distant or warm and engaging? Do your emails, texts, meetings, and calls motivate, inspire, engage, or enlighten—or are they just delivering information coldly without value, context, or proper framing? In what ways can you improve your communications with colleagues, employees, and clients?

4) ACCOUNTABILITY

If you don't hold individuals accountable, urgency is lost, and deadlines slide. If you don't keep yourself accountable as a leader, people lose faith in you and assume it's a "Do as I say, not as I do" environment. Trust is the first casualty when accountability is inconsistent or non-existent.

Consider these eye-opening statistics on accountability:[13]

- 93 percent of employees don't understand what their organization is trying to accomplish or how it matches their work.

- 85 percent of leaders don't define what their people should be working on, and an equal number of employees crave clarity.

- 84 percent of the workforce describes themselves as "trying but failing" or "avoiding" accountability, even when employees know what to fix.

---

13   Anne Loehr, "Why Accountability Is a Must for Teamwork and How to Create It," AnneLoehr.com, accessed November 2024, https://www. anneloehr.com/2017/06/08/accountability-a-must-for-teamwork/.

Those are strikingly high percentages, indicating that organizations have a massive problem with accountability. How can you improve accountability in your organization? Here are a few suggestions:

- Set clear objectives, key results, and performance indicators for any endeavor.

- Set clearly defined team and individual goals with incentives and penalties. The more specific your benchmarks, the easier it is to hold people accountable for reaching them.

- Break larger, long-term goals into smaller, short-term goals. Doing so makes it easier to identify specific, easily achievable steps and create a timetable to meet each step.

- When soft and hard deadlines are missed, have a constructive conversation about what prompted them to be forgotten, overlooked, or ignored. It should be a collaborative, not a negative, conversation.

- Focus on what happened and why. Avoid definitive action until you fully understand the situation. It may be your fault for failing to set them up for success.

- When deadlines are met and goals are achieved, recognize and celebrate them.

- Finally, remember that no individual, including yourself, is more important than the organization's mission. Hold everyone accountable.

Accountability can ensure things get done. It can also spur rebirth and renewed success. In 2008, Starbucks found itself on the ropes. During the start of the Great Recession, six hundred of their stores closed, and profits fell by 28 percent. The company, naturally enough, blamed the economic crash.

However, when Howard Schultz, the founder, returned as the coffee empire's CEO to hold leadership accountable, he had a different view. He pointed out that while leadership blamed their downturn on things beyond their control, they ignored what was within their power. He believed Starbucks had grown into an expensive and cumbersome bureaucracy in his absence and had lost its ability to pivot. Schultz quickly implemented a creative approach to rebuild brand trust and facilitate Starbucks's return to its roots. He invited customers to participate in the company's initiatives by submitting suggestions to his online "My Starbucks Idea" campaign. In its first year, seventy thousand new ideas were generated. Schultz's new approach helped Starbucks pull out of its slump.

Challenge Questions: How do you hold colleagues and employees accountable when they need to perform and be capable? How do you keep yourself accountable? How do others hold you responsible? Do you recognize when you have made a mistake? Do you immediately admit your mistakes and address them? How do you set clear expectations and hold individuals and teams accountable?

The Three C's for Measuring Performance

In the fourth quarter of Super Bowl LIV, the Kansas City Chiefs were down by ten points to the San Francisco 49ers. Time was running out, and a few players seemed like they were already resigned to a loss. Wide receiver Tyreek Hill, in particular, seemed down, and quarterback Patrick Mahomes took notice. He approached Hill and said, "I need you, man. Get your mind right and believe."

Mahomes calmed Hill down and got the rest of the team to adjust their attitudes. He pumped them up, saying, "Hey, this is going to be special. They'll talk about this forever, baby. They are going to talk about this forever. If we keep rolling, it's going to be special!" And because the team trusted him after all they had been through together, they soaked up his enthusiasm. For his part, Mahomes knew that if he could turn around the team's mindset, he had the potential to turn around the entire game. He knew his team. He knew what everyone could do. He knew how far he had to move the ball. So, he reached into his bag of tricks and pulled out a play that had worked for the team the previous year in the AFC Championship game.

The play was successful. The drive culminated with a touchdown. Building on newfound confidence, the Chiefs scored again. By the end of the quarter, the Chiefs had scored twenty-one points and won the game by eleven.

The Chiefs' victory that day happened for one reason. They won because of the culture of trust Mahomes had established with his teammates. When he abruptly called a play they hadn't done in over a year, everyone was with him and ready to execute. The result was unforgettable, but it was not completely unforeseen. With preparation and trust in leadership, success can become inevitable.

Those magical few minutes only came about because Mahomes had worked hard to gain his team's trust and confidence during the earlier part of the season. In particular, he had demonstrated three underlying levels of performance—what I call the *Three C's for Measuring Performance*—that every leader must bring into the arena with them 24/7:

1. Competency

2. Consistency of Competency

3. Comprehension of Competency

This powerful trio supports our 12 Elements of Trust at a foundational level, so let's explore each in more detail.

1) COMPETENCY

Mahomes always brought competency to the field, whether in practice or a game. He set a high level of performance that motivated others to do likewise. A business leader should do the same. Showing competence in business dealings and leadership demonstrates to your team that you can get the job done at a high level and conveys that you expect them to step up and do likewise.

2) CONSISTENCY OF COMPETENCY

Have you ever had a coworker who seemed to be a different person depending on what day it was? You probably, at some point, realized they were not very reliable. Maybe they would come into work unfocused and unmotivated or flip the script and show up excited and ready to get to work. You didn't know which personality would show up on any given day, so how could you trust them? Yes, we all have bad days, but we also should try to "get in the game" and be reliable and consistent at work. Achievers like Mahomes know the importance of showing up every day and giving it their all. The more a leader exhibits that kind of commitment and certainty of purpose, the more employees and colleagues will model that behavior.

3) COMPREHENSION OF COMPETENCY

Comprehension is the secret sauce to creating a culture of trust. It represents the ability to look at the whole of a situation, read between the lines, and find opportunities. That's what Mahomes did when he reached back to remember the play the Chiefs had successfully pulled off the previous season—and then recognized that same play might work in the difficult situation the team found themselves in that day, in the Super Bowl. Fully understanding his and his team's abilities and recognizing that something radical had to be achieved to turn things around, Mahomes took a comprehensive view that pointed him to a viable solution. Without that level of comprehension, the team may have faltered.

In other words, you can demonstrate competency and consistency, but if you don't understand what's happening, you're unlikely to hit on the solutions that will enable you to succeed. Think of the Starbucks leadership before Howard Schultz returned to head things up. They didn't fully comprehend the trouble they were experiencing. They also didn't understand what they needed to accomplish going forward to escape that trouble.

In short, they lacked *Agility*—the ability to be nimble to produce a successful outcome in any fluid situation. As previously discussed, Agility only comes to leaders that successfully master the Three C's—Competency, Consistency, and Comprehension.

Today, Agility is a prized commodity in leadership. As mentioned earlier, VUCA times have dominated our world. Shocks will keep coming in the form of pandemics, extreme weather events, economic downturns, wars, and elevated political turbulence. Leaders must be agile to navigate these shocks effectively in order to succeed.

In the past few decades, we've seen some huge companies (think Kodak, Blockbuster, Toys "R" Us, and Sears) march in lockstep to their doom—not because change left them behind, but because management refused to deal with that change promptly. They lacked the comprehension of the oncoming storm and what was needed to protect themselves from instant obsolescence.

Great leaders have that comprehension. Their understanding of a situation is frequently off the charts, allowing them to pivot on a dime if necessary. That's what Patrick Mahomes did in the fourth quarter of the Super Bowl, and that's what any leader can do by putting the Three C's to work.

LEADING WITH TRUST

If your actions inspire others to dream more, learn more, do more, and become more, you are a leader.

—JOHN QUINCY ADAMS

The most influential person in my life faced enormous adversity. At fifty-two, she was diagnosed with cancer, died twice on the operating table, battled back, and survived. She returned to work within months of surgery, even though cancer had taken her voice box. She was on the phone daily, talking to clients and referring to her now radically different speech as her "Brooklyn accent," which was funny to everyone, except for those from Brooklyn. Her clients laughed with her and were put at ease. They were happy and relieved she had not lost her sense of humor.

That woman was my mother, whom I wrote about earlier in this book. She possessed such a powerful driving force that she faced death and overcame it. Her strong drive was always present in her work and in caring for her family, friends, community, and church. As a result, she created positive change throughout her life, achieving many firsts for women of her time despite her health challenges.

Her strength and determination exemplify the power that defines authentic leadership—a power you can harness. There's no reason you can't do what you set out to do when you walk through the door to your next meeting or, these days, when you turn on your camera. If you master The 12 Elements of Trust, you can achieve whatever you set out to do. *The 12 Elements of Trust for Achieving Peak Performance* will empower you to earn trust and elevate your leadership. Your confidence and success will be unmatched when you internalize and customize the twelve elements to your style and comfort level. Your team members will notice and gain confidence in your leadership as well as gain confidence in themselves.

Don't think about who you are today—think about the person you will become tomorrow with the knowledge gained from this book. One of my favorite quotes is from legendary author and playwright George Bernard Shaw, who wrote, "Life isn't about finding yourself. Life is about creating yourself."

You can change your behaviors and mindset to "create" the leader you want to become. I know because I've seen it happen. Trust makes the impossible possible. I've been fortunate to play a role in helping transform many organizations and individuals, guiding them to achieve higher levels of success and prosperity. It's always an exciting journey to experience.

As you go forward, I wish you great success in your leadership journey, leadership built on trust. Use the guidance and knowledge provided in this book as a starting point for building greater trust and improving your leadership skills. Look further into the ideas offered here and make them instrumental to your development. Use them to nurture your team's desire to win in business and in life. To further assist you and your team with your development, I invite you to visit New Amsterdam at ThinkNewAmsterdam.com. Here, you can explore all we offer to complement your leadership, negotiation, and sales development.

My mother ended all her meetings with, "Get back to work!" followed by a big smile. And so, in closing, and with a big smile, I'll leave you with, "Get back to work, *Leading with Trust*."